D1561126

# THE MUSICIANS LIBRARY
## VOLUMES ISSUED

*The Song Volumes, excepting ix, x, xix and xx, are issued in editions for High and Low Voice.
Price of each volume, paper, cloth back, $1.50; full cloth, gilt, $2.50. Prices include postage*

SELECTIONS FROM THE MUSIC DRAMAS OF
RICHARD WAGNER

# SELECTIONS
## FROM THE MUSIC DRAMAS OF
# RICHARD WAGNER
## ARRANGED FOR THE PIANO BY
## OTTO SINGER
### WITH A PREFACE BY RICHARD ALDRICH

THE
MUSICIANS
LIBRARY

# BOSTON : OLIVER DITSON COMPANY

### NEW YORK : CHAS. H. DITSON & CO.  CHICAGO : LYON & HEALY
### PHILADELPHIA : J. E. DITSON & CO.

[ PRICE: PAPER, $1.50; CLOTH, $2.50 ]

D. B. UPDIKE, THE MERRYMOUNT PRESS, BOSTON

# CONTENTS

*[ From a Family Group, the last Photograph taken from Life ]*

# RICHARD WAGNER
## AND
## HIS MUSIC DRAMAS

THE "Wagner question" that ravaged the musical world for half a century and more has finally been put to rest; and through the acceptance of Wagner's works by the musical public of the whole world has been achieved the end for which the composer fought and suffered for a lifetime as probably no musician before him ever fought and suffered. The seventy years of Wagner's life were marked by a remarkable development, an increasing self-revelation. The career of most composers can be divided into periods; their works can be grouped together to represent successive styles. But of the eleven operas and music dramas that constitute practically the sum of Wagner's achievement, each represents a phase of its own, a new step in the progress of his advance. From his "youthful indiscretion," *Die Feen*, to *Tristan*, *Götterdämmerung* and *Parsifal* there is a steady progress toward higher ideals. Each work marks a significant advance not only in ideal but in style and technical power.

Wagner differed from most of the other great ones in music in showing as a child little of the specifically musical precocity that would foreshadow his coming greatness. His life was one of such turmoil, adventure and suffering as few have passed through; of such aggressiveness, tenacity and intellectual activity as only one possessed of an overmastering dæmon of genius could endure. He was born in Leipzig on May 22, 1813, the son of a police clerk, and the youngest of nine children. His earliest years were passed in straitened circumstances. He revelled in poetry, and had huge ambitions as a poet and as a Greek scholar—ambitions that later turned toward music. He was given a musical training, and made elaborate attempts in his salad days at musical composition; but none of them show the slightest

spark of genius, or trace of more than ordinary talent. At twenty he secured employment at Riga, in the opera house where his brother Albert was actor, singer, and stage manager, and where he gained his first technical acquaintance with the operatic stage. Here he composed two operas, *Die Feen* (*The Fairies*) and *Das Liebesverbot* (*Forbidden Love*), the latter of which was produced with disastrous results, which it no doubt eminently deserved. *Die Feen* he could not succeed in putting upon the stage; but it was produced five years after his death, and shows only a certain dexterity in treating pictorial stage effects, and is without a trace of musical originality.

His next few years Wagner spent as conductor of the opera at Königsberg and Riga, and in vain attempts to gain a foothold on the stage for his operas. Here he composed *Rienzi*, the first of his works that shows the true stuff that was in him. For this, as for all his other works, he wrote the libretto. He adopted an historical subject, which he treated in the grandiose, brilliant and glittering style of Meyerbeer. He hoped to secure its performance at the Grand Opéra in Paris; and so great was his confidence in the work that he set out for that capital in 1839, with his wife, and presented his claims to the director. In Paris he remained six years, quite unsuccessful in forcing his way upon the stage of the Opéra, and in circumstances of the bitterest poverty and disappointment; but these years were made notable by his composition of *Der Fliegende Holländer* (*The Flying Dutchman*). Meantime *Rienzi* had been accepted by the Royal Opera of Dresden, and Wagner returned thither to bring it out, in 1842. Its performance was a brilliant success, and led to the acceptance of *The Flying Dutchman* there, and Wagner's appointment the next year as conductor, which post he retained for six years. *The*

*Flying Dutchman* failed on account of its novelty of style and subject, and its originality of treatment; but undeterred by this, Wagner went on with the composition of *Tannhäuser* and *Lohengrin*, which marked still more radical departures from the accepted operatic style, and which carried him a long way on his road as an operatic reformer. The outbreak of the revolution of 1849, in which Wagner took a certain part, made necessary his flight from the Saxon capital, pursued by the police and barred from returning by a sentence of banishment.

In June, 1849, he took up his abode in Zurich, Switzerland, entering there upon a new and momentous period in his artistic development. He produced that remarkable series of literary works, essays theoretical and controversial, in which he elaborated and expounded his theories as to the true function of the lyric drama. At the same time he began to work on the great *Nibelung* trilogy, which was gradually expanded from a single music drama into four, and which first embodied his final views as to the proper relations between music and the drama, the true sources from which the musical dramatist should draw his inspiration, —the myths of the Teutonic people,—and the ethical function of the highest type of dramatic literature. Again in straitened circumstances, he was kept from shipwreck and despair by the beautiful sympathy and helpful generosity of Franz Liszt, who supported him with his words of encouragement and admiration, with frequent gifts of money, at the same time producing his works at the court theatre of Weimar, and otherwise making propaganda for them. While still engaged upon the *Nibelung* trilogy, hopeless of ever seeing it staged and performed, he laid aside the score to compose *Tristan and Isolde* in 1857–1859. He was called to Paris in 1861 to produce his *Tannhäuser*, of which he had to witness the uproarious fiasco. There were a few years more of wandering and of suffering, during which a proclamation of amnesty allowed him to return to Saxony, and in the course of which he took up and completed his comic opera, *Die Meistersinger von Nürnberg* (*The Mastersingers of Nu-*

*remberg*). These were dark days. Wagner was at the end of his resources, in despair of ever gaining the recognition he felt he deserved, and he saw nothing before him to bid him hope for the future. As a bolt from the blue came a message of hope from King Ludwig II of Bavaria, who, at eighteen years of age, had just ascended the throne, and whose first act was to send for Wagner and offer him the position and the power that he had yearned for all his life to carry out his projects. At Munich he finished the *Nibelung* trilogy and began on *Parsifal*, the conception of which had first come to him many years before. His work and his enjoyment of his royal patron's favor were interrupted by popular dissatisfaction and the intrigues of hostile musicians, which resulted in his retirement, finally, to the little hill town of Bayreuth. Here, after much laborious effort and many disappointments, he succeeded in erecting the famous Festival Playhouse for the performance of his works in accordance with his own ideals,—a desire that had obsessed him since he had arrived at the final formulation of his musico-dramatic theories years before. Here, in 1876, he first produced in its entirety the great *Nibelung* trilogy; and six years later his last and crowning work, *Parsifal*. He died on February 13, 1883, in Venice, whither he had gone in search of health, having accomplished such a revolution in the art of dramatic music as no man before him had ever seen brought to pass.

## II

WAGNER's principles, toward which he first began to grope in *The Flying Dutchman*, and which he fully formulated in the later series of his works, *Tristan, The Ring of the Nibelung, The Mastersingers* and *Parsifal*, are based on a reversal of the hitherto existing conception of what the opera should be. He demanded that the opera should be a drama, first and foremost, and that its chief purpose and its chief interest should lie in an unfolding of the dramatic idea upon which it is founded. To accomplish this, music should be, not the chief end, as it was in the current form of opera, but a means to an end, namely, the exposition of the dramatic effect. To this end all the resources of music, poetry, declamation, action, and stage picturing must unite, each sacrificing some of its own individual importance for the benefit of the greater good. Instead of music being an opportunity for the display of the vocalist's powers, a source of constant interruption to the dramatic progress, as in the arias and cavatinas of the accepted form, it should be employed to heighten the emotional power of the drama and contribute to the continuity and impressiveness of the whole. Instead of being distributed in various disconnected pieces of definite and circumscribed form, determined by considerations solely musical, it should be an uninterrupted accompaniment of the action, dependent for its form and texture wholly upon the course and the exigencies of that action; illustrating, expounding and emphasizing all the emotions, passions, promptings and dramatic incidents upon the stage, characterizing the personages, and interpreting their underlying motives. This task Wagner entrusts chiefly to the orchestra, which his genius raised to a potency and variety of expression before only dimly perceived. His music is evolved from numerous melodic phrases, usually short, of pregnant and significant form and harmonic basis, called leading motives. Each is associated with some particular meaning,—a character in the drama, some attribute of a person or thing, some ethical or emotional factor that has a prominent place in the dramatic whole. From these leading motives he elaborates a vast symphonic structure, of ever-changing form and substance, that serves as an exposition of the dramatic action as it is unfolded. The personages of the drama declaim, above this, a sort of melodious recitative or "endless melody,"—speech, as it were, heightened and intensified in its expressive power. All these elements are united into one organic whole.

### III
### RIENZI
*Rienzi*, Wagner's third opera, was, until *The Fairies* was produced in 1888, the earliest of his dramatic works known to the public, and properly counts as the starting-point of his successful career upon the lyric stage. In it he still entertains the conventional ideals of grand opera current in the first half of the last century,—ideals based upon the theatrical models of Meyerbeer and Scribe and the art of the Grand Opéra of Paris. Its subject is historical, and its treatment is based on Bulwer's novel *Rienzi*; its music is operatic, rhetorically pompous, brilliant, without great sincerity, but with a certain rude strength.

*Rienzi's Prayer* (*Almighty Father, look from Heaven*). In the last act, the curtain rises upon Rienzi alone in a hall of the Capitol at Rome. The insurrection under his leadership has been met with counterplots of the nobles and priests, and the popular tide has turned against him. He is aware of the dangers that surround him on all sides, and utters an impressive prayer, imploring that what God had accomplished through him in championing the cause of the people may not be brought to naught. There is an extended orchestral introduction; the prayer is expressed in a broad and noble melody (frequently introducing that "essential turn" so characteristic of the earlier Wagnerian melody) that plays a prominent part in the overture.

### THE FLYING DUTCHMAN
Wagner conceived the idea of *The Flying Dutchman* while he was on his voyage in a sailing-ship from Riga to England in 1839. He had already become acquainted with Heine's version of the legend, and the sea-scenes of the voyage impressed it more deeply on his imagination. The result was the first of his operatic works to show the true stamp of his genius. There are magnificent pictures of the ocean in the overture; the vigorous life of the Norwegian seafarers is depicted with an al-fresco freedom. The tragic gloom of the Dutchman, the mystic dreamings of Senta, give a strange and characteristic emotional color to the work. And though it cannot be ranked with Wagner's greatest productions, its imaginative power and strong and vivid coloring have given it a portion of immortality.

*Introduction to Act II, and Spinning Scene.* At the beginning of the second act we are shown a large room in the house of Daland, the sturdy Norwegian sea-captain, who has been making the acquaintance of the Flying Dutchman in the storm that has brought them both to land. His daughter Senta sits dreamily gazing on a picture of the stranger that hangs on the wall. She is surrounded by maidens, who sit and spin, singing the while of their wheels and their work, of their true loves who are at sea and of the wind that shall bring them speedily home, and now and again stopping to rally Senta upon her melancholy musings.

TANNHÄUSER

The mediæval legends of Tannhäuser and the minstrel knights of Germany first came to Wagner's attention in 1841. He at once saw in them material for his newly forming ideal of a national German operatic art, and developed them into an opera during the first year of his incumbency at Dresden. He used these legends, as he did others of a similar kind later, with the utmost freedom, and wrought out of them a drama of deeply poetical form and ethical import,—an opera that still remains, in the opinion of many, the most effectively and completely dramatic of any of his works. From his own point of view as a musician, however, *Tannhäuser* is but a milestone upon the road of his progress. It contains much strikingly vigorous and dramatic music,—dramatic in the true sense, and rising to the highest artistic level,—but it also contains cheap and tawdry strains of melody not above the composer of *Rienzi*. It shows little of the characteristic Wagnerian system of the later works; but it shows a great gift of characterization and of the use of music to express dramatic ideas, even within the limitations of conventional operatic forms.

*March from Tannhäuser* (*Entrance of the Guests into the Wartburg*). The Landgrave Hermann of Thuringia and his daughter Elisabeth stand in the great hall of the Wartburg, in the second act, to receive the guests invited to witness the minstrel knights' tournament of song. The guests enter in a brilliant company, make their obeisances to host and hostess, and gradually seat themselves. The orchestra plays, while this is going on, spirited, march-like music, introduced by crashing trumpet fanfares upon the stage. Yet Wagner is most urgent in his directions that this scene with its music shall not be treated as a march; that the entrance of the guests shall not be as a procession of the conventional sort, but that all shall take place in a natural and unstudied manner.

*Wolfram's Romance* (*O thou sublime sweet evening star*). In the last act Wolfram has just witnessed the return of the pilgrims from Rome without Tannhäuser, and has heard Elisabeth's prayer for peace and heavenly grace for the sinner. As she betakes her way up the ascent to the Wartburg, twilight falls, and Wolfram sings, to the accompaniment of his harp, an apostrophe to the evening star, and a summons for it to greet her when she leaves the vale of earth.

LOHENGRIN

The bondage of the conventional operatic forms was partially shaken off in Wagner's next opera, *Lohengrin*, which followed five years after the completion of *Tannhäuser*. Here he delved still further in mediæval legendary lore, in the great mass of the Grail legends which occupy so important a place in mediæval and earlier than mediæval Europe. *Lohengrin* embodied a conception of operatic form at that time new and original, and denotes a fine and subtle poetic sense in translating the original materials to the uses of the stage. There is extraordinary dramatic power in *Lohengrin*, and its music shows a great advance over that of *Tannhäuser* in the subtle distinction of its themes and their plastic development in dramatic characterization. It is more flowingly melodic than *Tannhäuser* or *The Flying Dutchman*, and, with much that is of the highest dramatic potency and strength, there is some of it that to-day seems sugary-sweet and cloying. In its form Wagner progresses a long way toward emancipation from the stencilled designs of the older opera. The vocal parts are more freely declamatory, the orchestra is entrusted with a more important function in interpreting the dramatic action and in giving atmosphere and color to the scene.

*Prelude to Lohengrin.* The prelude was, at the time, one of Wagner's most impressive achievements in orchestral writing, and still remains one of his masterpieces, the very embodiment of a celestial atmosphere, of the mystic character of the Grail, whose servant Lohengrin is. It depicts the descent of the sacred vessel filled with the Saviour's blood, borne by a group of angels. They gradually take definite shape before the onlooker's eyes, who thereupon sinks down in rapturous worship as at last the growing radiance of the music reaches its climax and the holy cup is uncovered and revealed to sight. The music dies gradually away in ethereal strains as the heavenly throng rises again and disappears on high.

*Elsa's Dream, and the Arrival of Lohengrin.* Summoned before King Henry the Fowler to answer the charges brought against her by Telramund and Ortrud, Elsa comes forward, as in a trance, and describes a dream she had, in which she saw a knight in glittering armor come to defend her from her traducers. Him alone she would have as her champion in the gage of battle with Telramund. The heralds step forth to summon the knight who will fight for Elsa of Brabant. Twice the trumpet call is repeated. Elsa kneels and prays for Heaven to send the promised knight; and, as she prays, her prayer is answered. Lohengrin is seen approaching upon the river, in a boat drawn by a swan. The throng of Brabant nobles greet him with wonder and delight, and amid a scene of indescribable jubilation, Lohengrin is brought to the river's bank and steps forward upon land.

*Bridal Chorus.* The third act opens upon the nuptial chamber of Lohengrin and Elsa, to which they are conducted by ladies of honor and the king himself, to the strains of a bridal chorus, one of the most familiar passages in all Wagner's works.

## TRISTAN AND ISOLDE

In despair at ever seeing his *Nibelung* trilogy brought to actual performance, Wagner interrupted his toil upon it in his exile at Zurich in 1857, "left his young Siegfried under a linden tree," and betook himself to the composition of a subject that had been seething in his brain for several years — that of the ill-fated loves of Tristan and Isolde, another of the mediæval epics of chivalry and passion to which his studies for *Tannhäuser* and *Lohengrin* had just introduced him. There is a strange story that an agent of Dom Pedro, the Emperor of Brazil, had come to him to commission him to write an opera for Rio Janeiro, and that in *Tristan and Isolde* Wagner produced what he thought was an easily intelligible and easily mastered work suitable for South American singers and audiences, and for ordinary German opera houses. As a matter of fact it is the most "advanced," the most difficult and complex of all his music dramas. He wrote it in a white heat of passion, in a perfect delirium of inspiration, without a thought of style or of his philosophy of the music drama into which, in his composition of *The Rhinegold*, *The Valkyr*, and the beginning of *Siegfried*, he had already entered and in which he was now completely at home. It is a stupendous piece of impassioned expression through music, in which the tones flow as a lava stream, and in which the elements of external description and inner feeling, as Mr. Henderson has put it, are skilfully combined. Here there is no trace of any of the older forms of operatic structure; but the fullest realization of all the freedom of Wagner's method is attained, — the most perfect organic union of poetic diction, music and action on the part of the singing actors and orchestral players.

*Introduction to Tristan and Isolde.* The prelude, another of Wagner's most impressive orchestral works, is charged with the deep yearning, the tumultuous passion of the luckless lovers, and its form is a perfect expression *in petto* of the main emotional outlines of the drama.

*Opening of Act II, and Love Duet.* The second act opens with a fiery orchestral prelude, depicting the suspense, the impatience of the two lovers to be reunited, their passion and the longing and joy of their love. The rising of the curtain shows us a garden before the chamber of Isolde. It is a summer evening. Isolde and Brangaene watch the departure of the retinue of huntsmen and hear the vanishing strains of their hunting-horns. Isolde extinguishes the torch,—the signal to her lover to come to her,—and summons him impatiently with the waving of her scarf. After the impulsive and jubilant meeting, they are seated on a bench in the garden, and sing a rapturous love duet, an apostrophe to the night and love, voicing their longing for separation from the world and from the light of day, for union in everlasting forgetfulness.

*Isolde's Love-Death.* In the last act Tristan lies at the point of death in the garden of his castle in Kareol. After long waiting and agony of spirit, he sees Isolde come to him at last. The lovers are reunited for a moment only, and Tristan dies. Isolde falls unconscious upon his body, while King Marke laments the hero's death; then rising majestically, and as though transfigured in grief, she sings, with eloquent exaltation, of her lover in a last farewell, finally sinking lifeless by his side; and the tragedy is fulfilled.

THE MASTERSINGERS OF NUREMBERG

*The Mastersingers of Nuremberg*, Wagner's only comedy, full of genial humor, of lovable and delightful characters, of knightly love and maidenly charm, with amusing contrasts and brilliant pictures of mediæval burgess life in Germany, was the product of the darkest, most desperate period of Wagner's career. It was the period of his greatest misery and despondency; of his flight through Germany to avoid his creditors, and of his continual failure to interest the public or the operatic managers in any of his later and greater works. The subject had been in his mind for near a score of years; but he did not carry it to execution till 1862, when he found refuge and opportunity at a friend's house in Zurich to work upon it. Nevertheless, it shows such a freshness and brilliancy of inspiration, a fecundity of melodic invention and a skill of combination and felicitous expression, as are scarcely to be matched in any of Wagner's other works. Its keynote is a lyric joy in life and love and art. As Cosima Liszt wrote of it once: "It has called up the Nuremberg of the Middle Ages, with its guilds, its poet artisans, its

pedants, its cavaliers, to draw forth the freshest laughter in the midst of the highest, most ideal poetry."

*Overture to The Mastersingers of Nuremberg.* The prelude to *The Mastersingers* is an elaborate tone poem, setting forth the chief elements entering into the comedy that follows. The dignity and substantial worth of the Mastersingers' Guild, as well as its somewhat self-conscious pedantry and its artistic narrowness, Walter's longing and impulsiveness and chivalrous passion, the smiling tenderness of Eva, are expressed unmistakably in music splendid and sonorous, lavishly melodious, rich and warm in harmony.

*Walter before the Masters' Guild* (*By silent hearth*). Brought up before the conclave of the Guild to prove his title to membership in it, that he may become an aspirant to Eva's hand under the conditions laid down by her father, Pogner, Sir Walter von Stolzing sings a song in which he answers the question as to his artistic training, giving the poems of Walther von der Vogelweide and the coming of spring as the sources of his musical inspiration—the song *By silent hearth*. This song by no means pleases the Mastersingers, beautiful though it is, because it departs in many respects from their rules.

*Quintet* (*Dazzling as the dawn*). In the third act are gathered together in the house of Hans Sachs, besides Sachs himself, Walter, whom Sachs has sheltered over night after frustrating his attempt at an elopement; Eva, who has come on the pretence of having an ill-fitting shoe made right, but really to get sight of her lover; Magdalena, her duenna, who has come to fetch her, as well as to get sight of her own lover, David, Sachs's apprentice boy, who is preparing for the festival of St. John's Day, and to whom Sachs gives his freedom as a member of the Guild. Then and there they all unite in singing their respective joys in a quintet of ravishing melodious beauty and tonal color, of marvellous skill in part writing, and of absolute fitness to the dramatic and emotional situation. It prompts the wish that Wagner might oftener have been untrue to the artistic principle that estopped him from the writing of vocal ensemble pieces as destructive of dramatic verity.

*Walter's Prize Song (Gleaming at morning in dawn's rosy light).* In the last scene of the last act Walter steps forth in the assemblage of the Guilds and people of Nuremberg celebrating the feast of St. John. The contest in singing for Eva's hand is the business of the occasion. He will make good his claim, after the ridiculous fiasco of Beckmesser in singing a song that is not his own. Sachs interrupts the people's laughter at his discomfiture to tell them that the author of the song will prove its merit. Walter sings it—a melody that has frequently been heard earlier in the opera—in all its perfect beauty, glorifying Eva in paradise. For this he is adjudged worthy of a place among the Mastersingers, and of the bestowal of Eva's hand.

## THE RING OF THE NIBELUNG

Wagner's *magnum opus*, the trilogy of *The Ring of the Nibelung*, occupies the place of greatest importance in Wagner's life, both for what it is and for what it represents in his artistic development and his struggles to arrive at a complete expression of his aspirations. He was engaged upon it, all in all, for well-nigh seventeen years, though those years saw many interruptions to its progress. In 1848 he began it as a single drama, to be called *The Death of Siegfried*. As he worked upon it, its scope grew in his mind. He first saw the necessity of a preliminary drama, to be called *Young Siegfried*, but there soon came to him the conviction that a still greater expansion of the treatment was necessary to make all intelligible, and by the end of 1849, the first year of his exile, he had decided upon the form of a great trilogy of three dramas with an introductory drama, or prelude, as we now have it,—*The Rhinegold, The Valkyr, Siegfried, The Dusk of the Gods*. The material for this great work he derived from two sources—the national Teutonic epic of *Das Nibelungenlied* and the records of Norse mythology contained in the Icelandic Eddas and the Volsunga Saga. From these vast storehouses of story Wagner extracted, as was his wont, only some of the most salient figures and incidents, which he shaped to his dramatic uses with the marvellous skill and insight that made him one of the greatest of dramatists. He has made out of the maze of complicated and conflicting narratives a story of broad lines and austerely simple development; from the vast throng of the mediæval chroniclers' characters he has chosen a few commanding figures of gods, dwarfs, nixies and men. Of their doings he has constructed a colossal world-tragedy, ethical in its significance, portraying in its movement the conflicting powers of world-forces, elemental types of humanity and ideals of human aspiration, the immutable laws of righteousness and retribution. The vast scheme is carried out with unfailing grandeur and dignity of conception. It is the logical execution of all Wagner's elaborate theories as to the proper subject, the proper treatment of the lyric drama. The music shows his first definite and complete employment of his leading motives, of the perfect organic union of declamation and the symphonic expository music. Vast as is the number of leading motives that he uses in the trilogy, there is scarcely one of them that is not a striking example of the philosophy of musical expression. They are full of point and pith in their melodic outline, of pregnantly significant harmony. They are plastic, and offer an infinite opportunity to the resources of Wagner's genius for musical elaboration, for combination, for the expression of shades of meaning, and to follow the drama through all the ramifications of its development. In *The Ring of the Nibelung*, as one of his biographers has truly said, Wagner set himself beside the Greek dramatists.

*Storm Scene, and Entrance of the Gods into Walhalla.* The last scene of *The Rhinegold* shows the great castle of Walhalla completed, the giants who built it satisfied with the payment of the Nibelung's gold instead of the fair goddess Freia. The gods and goddesses are ready to enter into possession. But heavy mists still surround it. To clear them away Donner, the storm god, swings his hammer; a tempest, with thunder and lightning, follows; when it clears, the castle is seen bathed in the light of the setting sun, with a rainbow bridge spanning the intervening valley. Over this the celestial company walk in solemn procession, to grandiose measures in the orchestra.

*Siegmund's Love Song* (*Winter storms have waned*). In *The Valkyr*, first drama of the trilogy, Siegmund, having been sheltered in Hunding's hut from the storm, is seized with a passion of love for Sieglinde, captured and held captive by Hunding as his wife. This growing passion bursts out in an impassioned love song as the two are left alone after Hunding has gone to rest, hymning the power of Spring, who frees from the bonds of Winter his "bridal sister," love.

*Ride of the Valkyrs*. The Valkyrs are daughters of Wotan, whose duty it is to lift heroes fallen in battle upon their horses and bring them to Walhalla, to join the band fighting for the perpetuation of the power of the gods. With warlike cries they ride through the storm and clouds. In the beginning of the third act of *The Valkyr* they are gathering on a mountain peak before their return to Walhalla. The orchestral prelude depicts their wild riding as they approach; we hear the galloping of their horses in the orchestra, and the untamed nature of these warlike sisters is graphically portrayed.

*Wotan's Farewell and Magic Fire Scene*. Wotan, in the last scene of the last act, has decreed as a punishment for his disobedient daughter Brünnhilde the loss of the divine attributes he has bestowed upon her and her degradation to the lot of an earthly woman submitted to the will of her husband. He will put her into a deep slumber; the first man who comes by to awaken her shall possess her. But, yielding to her entreaties, he consents then to surround her with a wall of fire impenetrable to all save the greatest of heroes who has never known fear. Thus as a mortal woman she will not become the "plaything of scorn." After the disappearance of his rage, Wotan's long farewell to Brünnhilde is full of tenderness and of memories of past happiness. Its melody is of broad and noble sweep; and the orchestra gives special prominence to the flickering motive of

Loge the fire god, and the motive suggesting the slumber that is soon to enwrap her.

*Siegfried forging the Sword*. Siegfried, the young hero without fear, brought up in a cave in the forest by Mime, is the only one who can forge together the broken pieces of Nothung, the irresistible sword, by which alone the dragon Fafner, who guards the Nibelung treasure, can be slain. After repeated futile attempts on the part of Mime to accomplish it, Siegfried, impatient to possess himself of the sword, though ignorant of the blacksmith's craft, seizes the fragments, files them to powder, melts them, casts them anew and finishes the good blade from the rough casting with hammer and anvil. At his work he sings the boisterous song, "Nothung, Nothung, conquering sword!" telling of the blowing bellows, the glowing flame, the showering sparks, and then of the hammer that shapes the trusty sword.

*Morning Dawn and Siegfried's Rhine Journey*. In the prologue of *The Dusk of the Gods*, after a scene in which the three Norns spin the fate of the world in the night, day breaks upon the mountain top where Siegfried had found Brünnhilde and where in a glen they had been reposing in happiness. The coming of the dawn is shown by an orchestral interlude of wonderful pictorial beauty. There is a farewell scene between the two, and Siegfried departs with the horse Grane down the Rhine, to new deeds of valor. His departure and his Rhine-journey are signalized by a long descriptive orchestral movement compounded of numerous themes significant in this connection, and full of life, color and the hope and energy of the youthful hero.

*Scene of the Rhinedaughters*. At the beginning of the third act the three Rhinedaughters are seen swimming about in the river. They lament the loss of their gold, which once made radiant all the gloomy depths of the stream, in a beautifully melodious trio with an accompaniment as of flowing waters. Siegfried appears, and they beg him to return to them the ring he wears, made of the stolen Rhinegold. He disdains them at first, but finally is disposed to gratify them, till they threaten him with dire consequences if he does not, whereupon he declares that he will not be moved by threats, and refuses them. Prophesying evil, they disappear.

*Siegfried's Funeral March.* Evil soon comes. Hagen and the clansmen of Gunther gather for the hunt; and while they rest, they persuade Siegfried to entertain them with the story of his adventures. When he comes to the part he played in winning Brünnhilde,—whom subsequently through the magic arts of Hagen he has forgotten, and has helped Gunther to gain as his bride,—Hagen, Gunther's half brother, as though in revenge for treachery on Siegfried's part, kills the hero by a spear-thrust in his back. In consternation and gloom the assembled warriors lay him on his shield and bear him away. The orchestra plays as the gathering moves on its way music of the loftiest tragic power and most heroic mould, as a lament for the hero's death. Called commonly a funeral march, it is rather a mighty dirge, a summing up of his character and achievements in tones.

PARSIFAL

Like its predecessors, *Parsifal* shows a new departure in style from what Wagner had done before it. It stands by itself in its subject and treatment. It is a religious drama, based upon ethical and philosophical considerations. It conveys deep symbolisms through many of its characters and incidents. And in its general form and substance it is invested with a solemnity and a seriousness that make it merit Wagner's appellation, a "sacred festival play," and unfit it for ordinary performance in the repertory of ordinary opera houses. This drama, too, was derived from the Grail legends of the morning of European civilization whence he obtained *Lohengrin.* But in it, perhaps more than in any of his other works, he has ennobled and transfigured the material with which he wrought. In the music of *Parsifal* Wagner has interpreted with marvellous skill and effectiveness the noble and beautiful story that he has put upon the stage. Less spontaneous than that of *Tristan* or *The Mastersingers*, less rugged and grandiose than that of *The Ring of the Nibe-*

*lung*, it is nevertheless of a golden beauty, reaching heights that even he did not before attain in the utterance of impassioned agony and suffering, of celestial calm, of mystical exaltation of spirit. The drama deals with half metaphysical problems of sin and redemption, with strange contradictions in ethics and psychology. Its characters are beings of another order than ours, of another age of the world, of other ideals; but, through his music, Wagner has breathed into them the breath of life, and has set a thrall for his hearers in the magic accents of his music that few can resist.

*Prelude to Parsifal.* The prelude initiates us into the mood of solemnity and mysticism that pervades the drama. Three themes form the material out of which it is composed, and these are elaborated into an eloquent proclamation of aspiration and suffering, mounting aloft at first in celestial harmonies, then depicting yearning, striving and lamentation, through various thematic inflections of drastic discords, with "wonderful transfiguring chords of the seventh that flash in between," to quote the words of Albert Heintz.

*Parsifal and the Flower Maidens.* In the second act Parsifal, having left the castle of the Grail without initiation into its mysteries, comes to the castle of Klingsor the magician, and enters the entrancing garden peopled with beautiful damsels, for the enticement and destruction of the pure. In the midst of the embowered loveliness these maidens ply him with their alluring arts, now beseeching him to yield to them, now imploring, now bantering, now scolding. The music is all full of grace, of witchery and of charm, the melodies seizing, the rhythms insinuating, the harmonies like the shifting play of iridescence.

*Good Friday Spell.* In the third act Parsifal returns, after many wanderings, to the domain of the Grail, heavily burdened with grief and despondency. Gurnemanz and Kundry are there; the former calls upon him to remove the black armor that he wears. As Parsifal looks about him, he notices for the first time the smiling beauty of the fields and woods, and asks about it. Gurnemanz tells

# RICHARD WAGNER

him it is the spell of Good Friday,—the sinner's repentant tears bestrew the field and mead, all creation rejoicing to trace here the Saviour's love. It is a sustained passage of matchless lyric beauty, in which all the voices of the orchestra sing as in an uplift of ecstasy.

*Richard Aldrich*

## PROGRAM NOTE
### TO THE "TRISTAN" PRELUDE, WRITTEN BY THE COMPOSER

*The love story of Tristan and Isolde comes to us from very early times, appearing in some form in the poetic lore of every language of mediæval Europe. Tristan, though he dare not avow his own passion for Isolde, seeks her hand in marriage for his uncle, King Marke, whom he serves as faithful vassal; and she, constrained by her own love for the knightly suitor, must powerless follow him to be the bride of his lord. But the jealous goddess of love avenges herself for her downtrodden rights; for through an ingenious blunder the young pair drink a love-potion, which, according to the custom of the times, was destined by the careful mother of the bride for the couple united by reasons of state alone. Their passion blazes into a sudden flame, and they realize that they belong to each other. Now comes boundless yearning—the longing, the joy, the misery of love; the world, power, fame, honor, knighthood, fealty, friendship, all are scattered like an unsubstantial dream. Only one thing remains,—desire, which, ever new-born with thirst and languishing, nothing can still. There is but one release,—death, extinction, the sleep which knows no waking.*

*The composer in choosing this subject for the introduction to his love-drama felt himself in the peculiar and unrestricted realm of music; and since to exhaust the subject was impossible, he had to set his own limitations of treatment. He therefore planned a single vast crescendo, swelling up by gradual degrees from the most timid avowal, the gentlest attraction, through painful sighs, hopes and fears, torments and desires, joys and griefs, to the mightiest effort, to the strongest travail by which the immeasurable yearning of the heart seeks to find an outlet to the sea of endless love's delight. In vain! Helpless the spirit sinks back faint with desire—with desire that knows no realization, for every realization is but fresh desire—until in the final exhaustion, there dawns upon the failing vision the foreshadowing of realization's highest bliss. It is the rapture of dying, of negation, of the final release into that wonderful realm from which we stray farthest when with stormiest striving we try to penetrate its confines. Shall we call it death? Or is it the dark wonder-world, out of which, as the legend tells us, ivy and vine in closest embrace grew on the grave of Tristan and Isolde?*

[FOR FACSIMILE SEE FACING PAGE]

*Autograph Facsimile of close to the "Tristan" Prelude composed in 1859 for a Concert Performance at Paris*

# BIBLIOGRAPHY

## *In English*

CHAMBERLAIN, Houston S.: Richard Wagner. Translated by G. Ainslie Hight. London, 1897

FINCK, Henry T.: Wagner and his Works. 2 vols. New York, 1893

HENDERSON, W. J.: Richard Wagner. New York, 1901

JULLIEN, A.: Life and Works of Wagner. 2 vols. Translated by Florence P. Hall, with an introduction by B. J. Lang. Boston, 1892

KOBBÉ, Gustav: Life and Works of Wagner. 2 vols. New York, 1890

KREHBIEL, H. E.: Studies in the Wagnerian Drama. New York, 1891

LAVIGNAC, A.: The Music Dramas of Richard Wagner. Translated by Esther Singleton. New York, 1898

NEWMAN, Ernest: A Study of Wagner. New York, 1899

WAGNER, Richard: Prose Works. 8 vols. Translated by William Ashton Ellis. London, 1892–1899

WESTON, Jessie L.: The Legends of the Wagner Drama. New York, 1896


## *In German and French*

CHAMBERLAIN, Houston S.: Das Drama Richard Wagner's. Leipzig, 1892
   Richard Wagner. München, 1896

CHAMBRUN, Le Comte de: Wagner, Traduction avec une introduction et des notes. Paris, 1895

DINGER, H.: Richard Wagner's geistige Entwickelung. Leipzig, 1892

ERNST, A.: L'œuvre de Wagner. Paris, 1883

GLASENAPP, C. F.: Das Leben Richard Wagner's. 2 vols. (*not complete*). Leipzig, 1894–1899
   Richard Wagner's Leben und Wirken. 2 vols. and Supplement. Leipzig, 1876–1882
   Wagner Encyklopaedie. 2 vols. Leipzig, 1891

HAUSEGGER, Friedrich von: Richard Wagner und Schopenhauer. Leipzig, 1892

JOHN, Alois: Richard Wagner-Studien. Bayreuth, 1889

JULLIEN, A.: Richard Wagner, sa vie et ses œuvres. Paris, 1886

KASTNER, E.: Wagner Katalog. Offenbach, 1878

KÜRSCHNER, I.: Wagner Jahrbuch. Stuttgart, 1886

LISZT, Franz: Dramaturgische Blätter, Vol. III: Richard Wagner. Leipzig, 1881

MUNCKER, Fr.: Richard Wagner. Bamberg, 1891

NOHL, Ludwig: Beethoven, Wagner, Liszt. Wien, 1874

OESTERLEIN, N.: Katalog einer R. Wagner Bibliothek. 4 vols. Leipzig, 1882–1895

POHL, Richard: Richard Wagner. Leipzig, 1883

SCHURÉ, Ed.: Le drame musical. 2 vols. Paris, 1875

TAPPERT, W.: Richard Wagner, Leben und Werke. Elberfeld, 1883

VOGEL, B.: Richard Wagner. Leipzig, 1883
   Richard Wagner als Dichter. Leipzig, 1888

WAGNER, Richard: Gesammelte Schriften und Dichtungen. 10 vols. Leipzig, 1887–1888, 2d edition
   Nachgelassene Schriften und Dichtungen. Leipzig, 1895

WEISSHEIMER, W.: Erlebnisse mit Wagner, Liszt, *u. s. w.* Stuttgart, 1898

WOLZOGEN, Hans von: Erinnerungen an Richard Wagner. Leipzig, *Reclam*

# BIBLIOGRAPHY

*Correspondence*

CORRESPONDENCE OF WAGNER AND LISZT. Edited by William Ashton Ellis, 2 vols. London

BRIEFWECHSEL MIT LISZT. 2 vols. Leipzig, 1887

BRIEFE AN UHLIG, FISCHER UND HEINE. Leipzig, 1888

BRIEFE AN ROECKEL. Leipzig, 1894

FÜNFZEHN BRIEFE AN ELISA WILLE. Berlin, 1894

ECHTE BRIEFE AN PRAEGER. Edited by Houston S. Chamberlain. Bayreuth, 1894

KASTNER, E.: Wagneriana I: Briefe Wagner's an seine Zeitgenossen. Wien, 1885

RICHARD WAGNER AN MATHILDE WESENDONK. Berlin, 1904

SELECTIONS FROM THE MUSIC DRAMAS OF
RICHARD WAGNER

# RIENZI'S PRAYER
## ALMIGHTY FATHER, LOOK FROM HEAVEN
### (Allmächt'ger Vater, blick herab)

From "RIENZI"
Act V, № 1

RICHARD WAGNER
*Transcribed by Otto Singer*

ML-840-3

# INTRODUCTION TO ACT II AND SPINNING SCENE

From
"THE FLYING DUTCHMAN"
(*Der Fliegender Holländer*)

RICHARD WAGNER
*Transcribed by Otto Singer*

ML-841-10

8

con Ped.

un poco riten.

# MARCH FROM "TANNHÄUSER"
## (ENTRANCE OF THE GUESTS INTO THE WARTBURG)

Act II, Scene IV

RICHARD WAGNER
*Transcribed by Otto Singer*

col Ped.sempre

Ped.

# WOLFRAM'S ROMANCE
## O THOU SUBLIME, SWEET EVENING STAR
(O, du mein holder Abendstern)

From "TANNHÄUSER"
Act III, Scene II

RICHARD WAGNER
Transcribed by Otto Singer

ML-843-4

# PRELUDE TO "LOHENGRIN"

RICHARD WAGNER
*Transcribed by Otto Singer*

ML-844-4

# ELSA'S DREAM, AND THE ARRIVAL OF LOHENGRIN

From "LOHENGRIN"
Act I, Scenes II and III

RICHARD WAGNER
*Transcribed by Otto Singer*

# BRIDAL CHORUS

From "LOHENGRIN"
*Act III, Scene 1*

RICHARD WAGNER
*Transcribed by Otto Singer*

M L - S 46 - 6

Tempo I

**Lento e languido**
(*Langsam und schmachtend*)

RICHARD WAGNER
*Transcribed by Otto Singer*

ML-847-6

*poco a poco ritenuto*
(allmählich im Zeitmaas etwas zurückhaltend)

# OPENING OF ACT II AND LOVE DUET

From "TRISTAN and ISOLDE"
*Act II, Scenes I and II*

RICHARD WAGNER
*Transcribed by Otto Singer*

M.L. 848-13

Tempo I

52

M.L.848-13

(The hunting-horns)

54

*Rallentando sempre poco a poco*
(Langsamer, und allmühlich immer langsamer)

Lento moderato, come prima
(Wieder mässig langsam)
tranquillo

60

# ISOLDE'S LOVE-DEATH
## (ISOLDENS LIEBESTOD)

From "TRISTAN and ISOLDE"
Act III, Scene III

RICHARD WAGNER
*Transcribed by Otto Singer*

ML-849-6

63

M L-849-6

64

# THE MASTERSINGERS OF NUREMBERG
## (DIE MEISTERSINGER VON NÜRNBERG)
### OVERTURE

RICHARD WAGNER
*Transcribed by Otto Singer*

ML-850-12

Animato ma sempre un poco largamente
(Bewegt doch immer noch etwas breit)

Moderato, Tempo I
(Mässig im Hauptzeitmass)

*più mosso*

Moderato (*Im mässigen Hauptzeitmass*)

*Poco a poco più f e più appassionato*
(*Immer bewegter im Vortrag und allmählich stärker*)

# WALTER BEFORE THE MASTERS' GUILD
## BY SILENT HEARTH
### (Am stillen Herd)

From
**"THE MASTERSINGERS OF NUREMBERG"**
*(Die Meistersinger von Nürnberg)*
*Act I, Scene III*

**RICHARD WAGNER**
*Transcribed by Otto Singer*

ML- 851- 6

# QUINTET
## DAZZLING AS THE DAWN
### (Selig wie die Sonne)

From
"THE MASTERSINGERS OF NUREMBERG"
*(Die Meistersinger von Nürnberg)*
*Act III, Scene IV*

RICHARD WAGNER
*Transcribed by Otto Singer*

ML-852-4

# WALTER'S PRIZE SONG
## GLEAMING AT MORNING IN DAWN'S ROSY LIGHT
### (Morgenlich leuchtend im rosigen Schein)

From
"THE MASTERSINGERS OF NUREMBERG"
*(Die Meistersinger von Nürnberg)*
*Act III, Scene V*

RICHARD WAGNER
*Transcribed by Otto Singer*

ML-853-7

# STORM SCENE AND ENTRANCE OF THE GODS INTO WALHALLA

From
"THE RHINEGOLD"
(Das Rheingold)
Scene IV

RICHARD WAGNER
Transcribed by Otto Singer

poco a poco cresc.

*ff*

*p* marc.

*ff*

*mf* marc.

largamente

# SIEGMUND'S LOVE SONG
## WINTER STORMS HAVE WANED
### (Winterstürme wichen dem Wonnemond)

From
"THE VALKYR"
(Die Walküre)
Act I, Scene III.

RICHARD WAGNER
*Transcribed by Otto Singer*

ML-855-6

108

# RIDE OF THE VALKYRS

From
"THE VALKYR"
(*Die Walküre*)
*Act III, Scene I*

RICHARD WAGNER
*Transcribed by Otto Singer*

M.L.856-6

# WOTAN'S FAREWELL AND MAGIC-FIRE SCENE

From
**"THE VALKYR"**
*(Die Walküre)*
*Act III, Scene III*

RICHARD WAGNER
*Transcribed by Otto Singer*

Molto animato
*(Sehr bewegt)*

PIANO

ML-857-14

126

Pedale tenuto sin'al fine

*ppp*

# SIEGFRIED FORGING THE SWORD

From "SIEGFRIED"
*Act I, Scene III*

RICHARD WAGNER
*Transcribed by Otto Singer*

ML-858-11

Pesante e risoluto, non troppo Allegro
(*Schwer und kräftig, nicht zu schnell*)

138

*) The 𝅗𝅥 a little broader than the ♩ before.

# MORNING DAWN, AND SIEGFRIED'S RHINE JOURNEY

From
"THE DUSK OF THE GODS"
(Die Götterdämmerung)
Prologue

RICHARD WAGNER
*Transcribed by Otto Singer*

Molto tranquillo
(Sehr ruhig, ohne zu schleppen)

(Twilight)

ML-859-10

Allegro molto

* According to the close given in Humperdinck's concert arrangement.

# SCENE OF THE RHINEDAUGHTERS

From
"THE DUSK OF THE GODS"
(*Die Götterdämmerung*)
*Act III, Scene I*

RICHARD WAGNER
*Transcribed by Otto Singer*

Animato, ma moderato il tempo
(*Lebhaft doch mässig im Zeitmaass*)

sempre col Ped.

# SIEGFRIED'S FUNERAL MARCH

From
"THE DUSK OF THE GODS"
(*Die Götterdämmerung*)
*Act III, Scene II*

RICHARD WAGNER
*Transcribed by Otto Singer*

ML-861-6

166

MI-861-6

168

# PRELUDE TO "PARSIFAL"

RICHARD WAGNER
*Transcribed by Otto Singer*

ML-862-7

# PARSIFAL AND THE FLOWER MAIDENS

From "PARSIFAL"
*Act II, Scene II*

RICHARD WAGNER
*Transcribed by Otto Singer*

ML - 863 - 10

ML-863-10

# GOOD FRIDAY SPELL

From "PARSIFAL"
Act III, Scene I

RICHARD WAGNER
*Transcribed by Otto Singer*

Maestoso con moto
*(Feierlich bewegt)*

PIANO

ML-864-7

189

ML-864-7